Just Call Me Firebucket

Robyn Wheeler

Just Call Me Firebucket
Robyn Wheeler

Copyright © 2019 Robyn Wheeler

All rights reserved. No part of this book may be used or reproduced by any means, graphic, electronic, or mechanical, including photocopying, recording, taping or by any information storage retrieval system without the written permission of the publisher except in the case of brief quotations embodied in critical articles and reviews.

The views expressed in this work are solely those of the author and do not necessarily reflect the views of the publisher, and the publisher hereby disclaims any responsibility for them.

Certain stock imagery © needpic.com

ISBN: 978-1-7332891-2-2 (sc)
ISBN: 978-1-7332891-3-9 (e)

Printed in the United States of America

Fire*buck-et *n.* a small red-headed, freckle-faced child who throws a tantrum; a nickname given to the author, Robyn Wheeler, by her godparents; a 2-year-old child who cries, yells, and stomps her feet because her siblings left her behind.

Contents

Introduction vii

Poems, Etc.

Life Is What You Make of It 3
Don't Take It Personally 4
Existing Is Agony 5
Mother Teresa: Do It Anyway 6
Peace Within 8
10 Attitude Commandments 9
15 Things to Give Up 10
10 Powerful Affirmations That Can Change Your Life 11

Blogs

Ho'oponopono 15
My Random Thoughts 17
Forgiveness 19
Surrender 21
Attitude 23
Christmas Never Left Christmas 25
Holiday (and Everyday) Kindness 26
Conquering Anger 27
A Vicious Cycle 31
Got Phobias? 33
It's All Small Stuff—*April 2011* 35
Why Bad Things Happen to Good People 37
Pet Peeves 39
Choices 41
A Big Deal Out of Nothing? 44
Perception of the Mentally Ill 46
The Diagnosis 48

Syndromes You Didn't Know Existed 54
Santa Kills Six 57
The Ohio Man—*February 2012* 59

Stories

Just Call Me Firebucket 65
The Little Girl with the Snake 67
The *Los Angeles Times* 68
Oh, Skunk! 70
Grilled Children 71
Joe Smith 72
Happy Easter! Happy Easter! Happy Easter! 76
Pot Brownies 79
You're on the Air 81
Comedy Speech 83

About the Author 91

Introduction

Just Call Me Firebucket is a collection of my random thoughts. It contains some of the poems and blogs I have written during the years I struggled with depression, as well as some fun stories of things that have happened to me. It makes a great sequel to *Born Mad*; but if you haven't read *Born Mad*, you can still read *Just Call Me Firebucket* and it will make sense. You can also read *Just Call Me Firebucket* from any page. It does not have to be read from beginning to end.

Some topics in this book will make you think, some may make you cry, and others will make you laugh. In addition, I hope some of the passages in this book will be helpful, whether you are a person with mental concerns or know of someone with mental concerns. Either way, I hope you enjoy reading *Just Call Me Firebucket*.

I'm not a poem writer. Or a regular poem reader for that matter. But on occasion I do enjoy reading them. I never set out to write poems. These poems came to me at a whim and I wrote them to help others with depression and to help their family members understand mental disorders. The Poems section is short because there are not many poems, but I thought I should publish them anyway. These poems will make more sense if you are familiar with depression and its symptoms. I've also included some other writers' poems that I found helpful, and hope they will help you, too.

Over the years I've written many blogs. I don't have a blog anymore or a forum to write new ones, but I picked out my best blogs to share with you. Some are helpful and others make you think about how you live your life.

These blogs are written from my point of view from my experiences. They are solely my opinion and not a doctor's or therapist's opinion.

Poems, Etc.

Robyn Wheeler

Life Is What You Make of It

All of us are kind, yet we are all evil.

All of us are individuals, yet we are all one.

All of us care, yet we are all uncaring at times.

Life is simple, yet it is too complicated for many.

Nothing is black and white, but shades of grey instead.

Nothing is real; the only reality is in our minds.

It is all a dream, yet it all feels so real.

Are we really who we think we are? Or are we really who others think we are?

Or are we neither one?

All of us are the same, yet we are all different.

All of us exist; yet some are already dead.

We all fulfill a purpose, yet some don't realize their purpose until it is too late.

We are all unique, yet no one is more special than another.

Life is filled with contradictions, yet both sides are correct.

Life ... is what you make of it; it is not what you are made of.

Life ... is what you make of it; it is not what you are made of.

—Robyn Wheeler

Just Call Me Firebucket

Don't Take It Personally

Don't take it personally
When they anger and rage
When they sulk and cry
Don't take it personally
When they accuse you of being unfair
When they accuse you of hating them

Don't take it personally
When they feel entitled and
Demand they get their way
Don't take it personally
When they use sarcasm and insults

Don't take it personally
When they don't speak for days
And think life is out to get them

Don't take any of it personally
For it is not about you
It is about them
Their mental illness is not
Your personal problem
It is theirs

Don't take it personally
Love them anyway
And know it is not your fault
Don't take it personally
It is the nature of the beast
It is their imbalance
Making them act that way
And theirs to correct

Don't take it personally

—Robyn Wheeler

Robyn Wheeler

Existing Is Agony

Anger and anxiety prevail
Joy and peace are illusions
Confusion overrides logic, despair is always there

Pain and agony creep into every cell
Creating a wound time cannot heal

The few happy, joyful memories are nothing but a distant past
You are grounded in one place on earth yet lost nowhere in invisible space
Who am I? Why am I here?
Is everyone else as miserable as me?
No answers, only constant questions
Too much grey, too little black and white

Thoughts are painful, existing is agony
Ruined relationships, constant nightmares, longing for death
What is the point? Does anyone really care? I don't

Disappointment in people, including yourself
Getting better is a mystery, a fantasy, a myth
Feelings of worthlessness continually roll around on a never-ending movie reel
Always with the same ending

Control feels like something only others have
Being controlled, enslaved by imbalance, I want out
All that can be heard is the screaming voice inside my head

I didn't ask for it nor do I want it
I'm willing to do anything to feel better
If even just for a day

Nothing limits me in my quest
Except ... myself

—*Robyn Wheeler*

Mother Teresa: Do It Anyway

Mother Teresa was born in Albania in 1910. She spent years of her life as a Catholic nun dedicated to humanitarian work for the poor, sick, dying, and orphaned, carrying out numerous missions the world over for hospices and homes for people with HIV, leprosy, tuberculosis, and much more. She is now with the Lord she loved so much, but she left behind many wonderful words we can and should all learn from.

I ran across a poem by Mother Teresa that is very fitting, profound, and worthy of mention, especially in our society today where we seem to be obsessed with what we can gain and profit from, rather than what we can give to others without expecting anything in return. If everyone on earth took these words to heart and practiced them as much as they could, we'd be living in a very different world today.

Do It Anyway

People are often unreasonable, irrational and self-centered. Forgive them anyway.

If you are kind, people may accuse you of selfish, ulterior motives. Be kind anyway.

*If you are successful, you will win some unfaithful friends and some genuine enemies.
Succeed anyway.*

If you are honest and sincere, people may deceive you. Be honest and sincere anyway.

What you spend years creating, others could destroy overnight. Create anyway.

If you find serenity and happiness, some may be jealous. Be happy anyway.

Robyn Wheeler

The good you do today will often be forgotten.
  Do good anyway.

Give the best you have and it will never be enough.
  Give your best anyway.

In the final analysis, it is between you and God.
  It was never between you and them anyway.

—Mother Teresa

These words are tacked up on my office wall so I may reread them every day, letting the meaning truly sink in to my soul.

If you have trouble with anger or resentment, want revenge for past wrongdoings, or have difficulty making decisions in a precarious situation, remember these words by Mother Teresa—they may just help you become a better person.

Don't think posting this quote on the wall can help you? *Do It Anyway.*

Peace Within

I received the following poem as an email and was asked to pass it on to eight other women, which I did. However, I liked it so much and thought it appropriate for all of us on earth and in all situations, I thought I would share it here as well. Enjoy!

> *May today there be peace within.*
> *May you trust that you are exactly where you are meant to be.*
> *May you not forget the infinite possibilities that are born of faith in yourself and others.*
> *May you use the gifts that you have received and pass on the love that has been given to you.*
> *May you be content with yourself just the way you are.*
> *Let this knowledge settle into your bones and allow your soul the freedom to sing, dance, praise and love. It is there for each and every one of us.*
>
> —*Author Unknown*

How many of us are really and truly content with who we are? Are you happy to be you, even though you might be overweight or stressed out or don't have enough time for your hobbies or reading a good book? Are you really, really content and peaceful with who you are? I wasn't... for a long time. I hated myself for being not smart enough, not skinny enough, not good enough. In *Born Mad*, you'll read how disliking myself led to thoughts of suicide and almost destroying every relationship in my life. But there was a happy ending for me. And there is for you and your loved ones as well.

Robyn Wheeler

10 Attitude Commandments

I didn't write this and don't know where I found it, but I still have it in my files. I thought I would share it with you.

1. It is attitude, not aptitude, that governs altitude.
2. The purpose of existence is not to make a living, but to make a life.
3. A negative thought is a down payment on an obligation to fail.
4. You will seldom experience regret for anything you have done. It is what you do not do that will torment you.
5. Complaining is the refuge of those who have no self-reliance.
6. The ultimate cost of something is the amount of life that you will exchange for it.
7. Youth is not a time of life, but a state of mind. Wrinkles test the skin but never touch the soul.
8. People who have no worthwhile purpose in life are easy prey of anxiety.
9. The worst bankruptcy is the person who has lost enthusiasm.
10. Nobody can make you feel inferior; they must have your permission.

Just Call Me Firebucket

15 Things to Give Up

Again, I didn't write this nor do I know who did, but felt it was worth mentioning.

15 Things to Give Up

1. Doubting yourself
2. Negative thinking
3. Fear of failure
4. Destructive relationships
5. Gossiping
6. Criticizing yourself and others
7. Anger
8. Comfort eating
9. Laziness
10. Negative self-talk
11. Procrastination
12. Fear of success
13. Anything excessive
14. People pleasing
15. Putting others' needs before your own

Robyn Wheeler

10 Powerful Affirmations That Can Change Your Life

I didn't write this one either, nor do I know who did. But, again, felt it was a great thing to share with you.

1. I can achieve greatness.
2. Today, am brimming with energy and overflowing with joy.
3. I love and accept myself for who I am.
4. My body is healthy; my mind is brilliant/ my soul is tranquil.
5. I believe I can do everything.
6. Everything that is happening now is happening for my ultimate good.
7. I am the architect of my life; I build its foundation and choose its contents.
8. I forgive those who have harmed me in my past and peacefully detach from them.
9. My ability to conquer my challenges is limitless; my potential to succeed is infinite.
10. Today, I abandon my old habits and take up new, more positive ones.

Blogs

Ho'oponopono

Ho'opono-what? Yes, *Ho'oponopono*. It is an ancient Hawaiian practice of reconciliation and forgiveness. I was first introduced to this idea in November 2010 at an "I Can Do It!" Conference in Tampa, Florida, by author Marci Shimoff *(Chicken Soup for the Soul, Happiness for No Reason)*. *Ho'oponopono* is seen as a mental cleansing; a form of asking for forgiveness, forgiving others, and taking 100 percent responsibility for your actions, believing that peace and harmony can only be remedied and strengthened by confession and apology. And it's actually very easy; every day when you wake up or before going to sleep at night, repeat these words either aloud or to yourself:

> I'm sorry.
>
> Please forgive me.
>
> Thank you.
>
> I love you.

Many years ago, *Ho'oponopono* was only performed by members of clergy or priesthood. Today, modern versions have been updated to include families, family elders, or just one person wishing for peace and harmony. In addition, if you wish to extend this practice, you may also repeat the lovingkindness practice which is as follows:

May you be safe, happy, healthy and live with ease.

Just think of someone you know and love who you want to send good wishes to. You don't have to call them or tell them you've sent them these friendly, nonviolent thoughts;

just say their name and wish them the above thoughts. Pick one person every day to say *Ho'oponopono* and the lovingkindness practices, and see what happens to them and to you.

If you want to take this further, you may become certified in *Ho'oponopono*. To do so, go to Facebook and look up "Ho'oponopono certification Joe Vitale" or go to HooponoponoCertification.com/. You can become certified in a short time.

Robyn Wheeler

My Random Thoughts

1. There has to be a use for snot. I've suffered from pollen allergies my entire life and had attacks that would take down an elephant. I go through boxes and boxes of Kleenex tissues. And it is a waste and a shame to throw away all that snot. My body generates so much snot that I am convinced I would be rich if I could figure what to do with it. Can't we make fuel out of it? It has to be good for something!

2. Do deer know they are supposed to cross at that yellow sign with the picture of the jumping deer on it?

3. You know those signs that say "Watch for Ice on Bridge"? I watch for it and have even seen it, but then I don't know who to call when I do see it. What is the point of watching for it when you don't know who to tell that you saw it?

4. I think everyone should be born with one million dollars. What you do with it is your business, but it has to last you your entire life. If you use it all, then you have to go out and get a job. If you are smart and save or invest it, then you don't have to go out and find a job. Brilliant idea!

5. Women should not have periods. When they decide to have a baby, then they take a pill to have a period. End of unwanted and accidental pregnancies. Much better idea than being forced to have a period year after year and not wanting to get pregnant or have babies.

6. I've always wanted to be a veterinarian. I got my Bachelor's degree in Animal Science, but didn't have the grades, money, or desire to go through another four years of college at the very least. So I've found this

television veterinary show called The Incredible Dr. Pol on the *National Geographic Wild* channel. I've learned a lot from watching the show and thought, *Wouldn't it be great if I got school credits for watching the show? I could become a veterinarian just by watching TV!*

Robyn Wheeler

Forgiveness

Our society seems to be very unforgiving these days. In a world filled with perfectionists and the fear of making mistakes, we've become less tolerant of others as a whole and expect others to do as we do. This can be extremely damaging to those suffering from dysthymia or other mental/mood disorders. And forgiveness isn't something someone else can do for you. There are no step-by-step instruction manuals to learn how. It's just something you have to do on your own, by yourself, in your own way. If you fail to forgive, let go, and move on, you'll find you become resentful, bitter, negative, and paranoid—insisting that everyone else is purposely out to get you and make your life miserable. I know. I used to be that way.

As a Type A Perfectionist personality and a Dysthymic, I expected others to be that way too and saw my way of doing things as the only "right way" and the "only way." Today I know different as I have seen the error in my thinking, which you may read about in detail in my book *Born Mad*. Everyone on the planet has their own way of doing things. There is no one right way or correct way, only different ways. What works for you is correct; and if someone does something differently, it is correct for them as well.

No one is perfect. No one. Not even the so-called "perfectionists." Everyone makes mistakes, goof-ups, and blunders every now and again. We all live in glass houses, which means none of us should be casting stones at others. Forgive everyone for everything—their faults, miscalculations, and poor judgments—for all of us are flawed.

Forgive Jeffrey Dahmer, Charles Manson, and Richard Ramirez, as they are mentally worse off than you. They live (or lived) every day, in their own inner hell and are unable to get out. Day after day, for eternity here on earth, they live in a world inside themselves that most of us cannot comprehend. Forgive those who commit heinous crimes, as they "know not what they do." Wish them love, happiness, and peace on the other side so they can escape their inner prison. But most of all, do it for yourself, so you do not confine yourself to the same prison they do.

Forgiveness is something you do for yourself to feel peaceful and happy, and to let go and move on. To quote Dr. Wayne Dyer, "There are no justified resentments." None. You hurt only yourself when you do not forgive.

It took me years of living with a terrible attitude and resentment before I could forgive. In *Born Mad* I wrote about feeling stuck in "between a rock and a hard spot," unable to figure out how to forgive, not even knowing where to start.

But now that I have figured out how to forgive, let go, and move on, I *never* wish to go back to being unable to do those things. Forgiveness has been the key to my new attitude and positive outlook on life.

First step for me: forgiving myself. If you are unable to forgive yourself, you'll *never* be able to forgive others. For more help, read or listen to any of Dr. Wayne Dyer's wonderful books and CDs on spirituality.

Surrender

Surrendering means to give up possession of or power over; to give up voluntarily. The key to living an anger-free, happy, and peace-filled life is to surrender. Give up your need and want for total control and just let things happen. Not every aspect of your life is under your control, so surrender to the events and situations you are faced with on a daily basis.

Stop fighting and battling every little event that does not go the way you expected or wanted it to, as that path causes anger and feelings of entitlement. Realize that each day is special and unique, no two are the same, and your duty in life is to make the most of what is presented to you. Your life is not defined by what happens to you; your life is defined by how you handle the things that happen to you.

Days or events are not good or bad; only your perception of them makes something good or bad. Change your perception so you can *make* it a good day instead of *hoping you will have* a good day. No matter what comes your way, surrender to the force larger than you: the universe, a divine plan, God—whatever you want to call it. Just know you are not in control and what is being given to you is what is supposed to be; it is a part of your journey, your path, and your learning adventure while you are here on earth.

If you feel each day is difficult, that others have it easier than you, and that you are swimming upstream while everyone around you is swimming downstream, stop fighting your circumstances and challenging your environment to adapt to you. Life for us humans is about adapting to our environment and finding the positive in negative occurrences like natural disasters, physical and mental illness, traffic accidents, etc. Not every day of your life will unfold as you expect it to; rather, it will unfold the way it is going to unfold, with or without your permission and acceptance.

We can change only what we have control over; everything else is under someone else's control. The hard part is being able to tell the difference. You have control over how you react and what you say and do. You do not have control over what diseases you will be affected by throughout your life, nor do you have control over what others say and do. So surrender your control, want, and need for things to transpire your way and only your way. Be flexible, bend, and work with what is given to you, even if it isn't what you wanted. Events you perceive as bad just might turn out to be the best thing that ever happened to you.

So next time your car breaks down, your spouse doesn't fold the laundry the way you like it, you get a kidney stone, or maybe you didn't get the job you were hoping for, remember to ask yourself if you have control over that particular situation. If the answer is yes, then make the necessary adjustments to make it fit your desires; if the answer is no, accept what was handed to you, work with it, and move on. If you get angry over something you have no control over, you'll never find peace and happiness. Feelings of entitlement, demanding that you receive what you want, and wanting to be better or acquire more possessions than others have, is a sure way to stay angry every day of your life. For peace and happiness, release control, cherish what you are given, and surrender to the forces far bigger than you.

Robyn Wheeler

Attitude

While cleaning out some files the other day, I found a small piece of paper with the following written on it:

Attitude

> The longer live, the more I realize the impact of attitude on life.
>
> Attitude, to me, is more important than facts. It is more important than the past, than education, than money, than circumstances, than failures, than successes, than what other people think or say or do. It is more important than appearance, giftedness or skill. It will make or break a company ... a church ... a home.
>
> The remarkable thing is we have a choice every day regarding the attitude we will embrace for that day. We cannot change our past ... we cannot change the fact that people will act in a certain way. We cannot change the inevitable. The only thing we can do is play on the one string we have and that is our attitude... I am convinced that life is 10 percent what happens to me and 90 percent how I react to it.
>
> And so it is with you ... we are in charge of our attitudes.
>
> *—Charles Swindoll*

I love this piece and had no idea who the man was/is who wrote it so I decided to Google Charles Swindoll to see if he was someone of mportance. And yes, he is. Charles R. Swindoll is a Christian pastor, author, and educator. He founded the *Insight for Living* radio program and the Stonebriar Community Church in Frisco, Texas.

He's written numerous books, including *The Mystery of God's Will, Getting Through the Tough Stuff, Bedside*

Just Call Me Firebucket

Blessings, and *The Ultimate Book of Illustrations and Quotes*. In the future, I might read one, two, or several of those. For more information on Charles Swindoll, his books or *Insight for Living*, go to Insight.org or ChristianBook.com.

Robyn Wheeler

Christmas Never Left Christmas

Many Facebook fans are talking about how Americans need to put Christ back into Christmas. But Christ never left Christmas ... unless *you* took him out. Christmas isn't about how it is spelled, or even the fact that Jesus may or may not have been born exactly on December 25. Christmas is about how you treat others, the random acts of kindness you do, and your compassion for others.

This is America, and we cannot force Christ on anyone who doesn't want to believe or who has beliefs different from the Christian viewpoint. There are three types of business in this world: yours, other people's, and Gods. You are only entitled to your business. If others wish to say Happy Holidays or Season's Greetings, what's so wrong with that? What is so wrong with respecting the beliefs of others and letting them worship whom and in whatever way they see fit? You have control only over yourself, how you think, and how you act. Everyone else's thoughts and actions are beyond your control.

So don't get mad over others' not "putting Christ into Christmas." The only thing you should be concerned about is if Christ is in *your* Christmas. Christmas isn't about being Christian ... it is about being a human being ... a kind human being. We say "Peace on Earth" during Christmas time, *not* peace only for those who believe in Christ. *Not* peace for Americans only. *Peace on Earth* means just that: Peace for everyone, even if they don't believe what you believe. Much peace and happiness to everyone on earth.

Holiday (and Everyday) Kindness

The holiday season is for loving and serving others. It is not the time to be selfish, greedy, and egocentric. So, try these few things during the holidays while you are with your loved ones—even if they tend to annoy you!

- Say something nice and compliment others. If you can't say anything nice, don't say anything at all.

- Avoid catastrophizing. You know ... making a mountain out of a molehill. Enjoy the moment, the present day. Your unfortunate circumstance could change to a positive event overnight.

- Bless your enemies. Better yet, have no enemies at all. Even if someone might not like you, send them love, peace and happiness.

- Remember that giving is much more fulfilling than receiving. Give and be happy you are able to do it.

- Do something good—a random act of kindness—and don't expect anything in return. Not even a compliment or acknowledgment. Just give for the sake of giving.

- Remember we all have a purpose in life. Think about what you believe to be your purpose and do one thing every day to make that purpose expand.

- Remember God, His will, His love and forgiveness. Be happy for every day you are given.

Merry Christmas, Happy Chanukah, Seasons Greetings, Happy Holidays, and Happy New Year. May all of you be blessed with good health, peace, and happiness always.

Robyn Wheeler

Conquering Anger

If you are a perfectionist, demanding everything you do to be flawless, you are setting yourself up to get mad. If you expect others to never make a mistake or to complete tasks exactly the way you do, you are setting yourself up for failure. When your spouse, coworker or children fail to do things exactly the way you expect them to be done, you are setting yourself up for anger.

Why? Because you are causing your own frustration and anger, not to mention extreme harm to your loved ones. How? Because no one is perfect and no two people perform tasks exactly alike. My husband folds clothes that I prefer to be on a hanger. His military background instilled in him to fold towels and clothes a particular way. I used to get mad at him for folding clothes I wanted hung up. I expected him to do things "my way." When your spouse doesn't fold clothes like you do and an argument ensues because you said they didn't fold them "right," the argument is your fault, not theirs, due to your unrealistic expectations.

It took me years to learn this. What are you really doing when you tell a loved one they are not doing it "right" is that they are not as good as you, that they are not worthy of being loved, and that you are always right (therefore superior) and they are always wrong. But the reality is, it's all small stuff—all of it. Including how your clothes are folded, which way the toilet paper hangs on the roll, and waiting in line in traffic or the grocery store.

To compound the problem, anger is a vicious cycle. Anger shuts people off from the world and creates closed-mindedness—the inability to try new things. Angry people blame others for things that are their own fault and believe they know all they need to know. (I was one of these people for decades.) If a person is unwilling to try new things and believes they "know it all" already, that person will miss out on trying the very thing that can rid them of their anger. If you don't try something new, you won't get rid of your anger; and if you are angry you won't want to try something new.

In addition to that, as if that weren't bad enough, one angry moment leads to another angry moment. Anger doesn't fix things—it just leads to more anger. Anger is like fire: It spreads, if not put out quickly and efficiently. And there's the cycle. At some point, maybe when you hit your all-time low or "rock bottom," you'll be willing to do anything and everything it takes to move on, to grow and progress as a human being. At some point, you'll have to better your own life by being flexible and open-minded. Keep in mind that the definition of insanity is doing the same thing over and over again, but expecting different results. One cannot make progress when one refuses to change.

Remember, if you make decisions when you are mad, you will most likely make the wrong decisions. Staying calm, rational, practical, and willing to compromise (being flexible) will most likely fix whatever situation you became irate about.

So here are my challenges for you to help conquer your anger. Should everyone on the planet do and like the same things you do? Wouldn't that be boring if all 6 billion of us acted exactly alike?

♦ **See others as individuals with their own emotions, needs, wants and habits.** When I hear of parents who are angry at their children for not wanting to go to the same college they did, major in the same field, and join the same sorority, my stomach turns. The parent's anger is not the child's fault. The parents are creating their own anger by expecting their children to be exactly like them. See your children as their own people, with their own needs and desires. Let them live life on their own path;

don't force them to follow your path or the path you for some reason gave up for something else.

Next time you get mad because your child didn't clean his room the way you would have, or made the bed a little sloppier than you would have (or for that matter didn't make it at all), ask yourself: Is it really that important? Important enough to cause high blood pressure, arguments with your loved ones, resentment, and feeling ticked off all day long (or longer, if you are like I was and stayed mad for days, weeks, and months)? Is it really that important? Answer: No. Instead of insisting your loved ones copy you when doing chores, homework, bill paying, or whatever else you can think of, why not allow them do it their way? They might even learn something in the process. And you might, too.

♦ **Get rid of unrealistic expectations**. Instead of insisting on having things "your way," try adapting to your environment and other people instead. Unless, you are truly facing a life or death situation—being chased by a wild, angry grizzly bear, being diagnosed with a terminal disease, being traumatically injured in a car crash, etc.—it's all small stuff. Life will go on, even when you make mistakes; and those who hold no expectations of themselves or others will always be happier than those who have unrealistic expectations. Get rid of your expectations first. Your anger will subside after that, and only after that.

♦ **Acknowledge your faults and mistakes**. Don't make excuses or blame others. When something is your fault, own it. Admit to it, say you are sorry, and make the necessary adjustments. No one likes someone who never admits to any wrongdoing (again, unrealistic expectations controlling your actions and words).

♦ **Try new things**. Try food, sports, going someplace with friends, meditation, medications, new therapies. But don't say "I've tried it all and none of it works." Keep trying new things to rid yourself of anger. Besides, if you only do things one way, how do you know you won't like the new way better?

♦ **Think back on something that made you mad years ago**. Then ask yourself a few questions:

1. Was it really that important? (A life or death situation)
2. Did you make the situation better by getting angry?
3. Did this situation make such a dramatic change in your life that you still remember it today? If not, whatever situation you are facing today will most likely be a forgotten memory a year or two from now. One cannot make progress when one refuses to change.

Remember, if you make decisions when you are mad, you will probably make wrong decisions. Staying calm, rational, practical, and willing to compromise (flexible) will most likely fix whatever situation you became irate about.

Robyn Wheeler

A Vicious Cycle

Ridding yourself of anger may sound easy to some people. However, it takes a lot more than reading a book or taking a class to truly live anger-free. No one can do it for you, so one mustn't look outside themselves for solutions but search within instead. The biggest problem is that anger is a vicious cycle. Let me explain.

If an individual is angry, odds are, that person does not want to try anything new. They blame others for things that are their own fault and believe they know all they need to know (I was one of these people for decades.) If a person is unwilling to try new things and believes they "know it all" already, that person will miss out on trying the very thing that can rid them of their anger.

If you don't try something new, you won't get rid of your anger; and if you are angry, you won't want to try something new. In addition to that (as if that weren't bad enough), one angry moment leads to another angry moment. Anger doesn't fix things; it just leads to more anger. Anger is like fire: It spreads if not put out quickly and efficiently. And there's the cycle. At some point, maybe when you hit your all-time-low or "rock-bottom," you'll be willing to do anything and everything it takes to move on, grow and progress as a human being. At some point, you'll have to save your own life by being flexible and open-minded. Keep in mind that the definition of insanity is doing the same thing over and over again, expecting different results.

One cannot make progress when one refuses to change. Many people dislike change. I say, "Bring it on!" Change is necessary, and you may even find you like the change better than "the old way." So if you are angry, wondering why you can't shed those terrible thoughts and feelings, try—no, *dare*—to do something new. If it doesn't work, try something else. But keep going, until you do find that one method, that one strategy that helps you live anger-free.

Force yourself to break the cycle. It isn't easy. Nothing in life worth fighting for is easy. But if you want it bad enough, you'll find a way. The exciting news about this concept is that one day anger-free will lead to two, and two will lead to three, and so on. Now I know that the longer I go anger-free, the less likely I am to get mad in the first place.

Robyn Wheeler

Got Phobias?

Anxiety, in past years, contributed to my unhappiness and depression. The more anxious I was, the unhappier I was. And getting rid of anxiety is difficult for many people, not just me. As I studied various techniques on how to become happier and less anxiety-ridden, I came across *Overcoming Anxiety for Dummies* by Dr. Charles Elliott and Dr. Laura Smith. One of many subjects discussed in this book is phobias.

I suffered from many phobias in the past, including fear of insects, flying, and drowning. Being afraid of those things made me more afraid. And being more afraid made me *even more* afraid—which, I have now learned, is called *phobophobia* (to be afraid of fear).

As someone interested in phobias and able to tame many of my fears, I wanted to know how one acquires fears and how one can rid oneself of them (if at all possible).

Phobias, according to Elliott and Smith, *are excessive, disproportionate fears of a relatively harmless situation or thing. Sometimes, the phobia poses some risk, but the person's reaction clearly exceeds the danger.*

The top ten phobias named by Elliot and Smith are:

10. Dogs
9. Being alone at night
8. Thunder and lightning
7. Spiders and insects
6. Being trapped in small spaces
5. Flying
4. Rodents (animals: zoophobia)

Just Call Me Firebucket

3. Heights (Acrophobia)

2. Giving a speech

1. *Snakes!* (ophidiophobia)

You're most likely familiar with most or all of those above. But how about these?

Eisoptrophobia (fear of mirrors)

Lachanophobia (fear of vegetables)

Triskaidekaphobia (fear of the number 13)

Psychophobia (fear of the mind)

Trypophobia (fear of small things)

Gerascophobia (fear of growing old)

Atelophobia (fear of imperfection)

Okay, maybe I still have a small case of atelophobia! But who doesn't, right?

It was my intention to end this blog by including an actual number of existing phobias one could suffer from. You know, something like "178,348 known phobias exist today." And I did, in fact, find a list on the Internet, but it would've taken forever to count them all. The list of phobias starting with the letter *A* alone was several pages long.

It was then I realized the number of possible phobias is infinite, never ending. One could be afraid of paper or computers, or sticky notes and correction fluid, or roses, or other fragrant smells. The list goes on, there's no way to count. This blog has no hidden meaning or message. No profound thought at the end. It is merely something that might interest you.

Or maybe not... if you have *centophobia* (fear of learning new things)!

Robyn Wheeler

It's All Small Stuff
April 2011

For years prior to my dysthymia diagnosis, I got mad at anything and everything. If some event during the day did not go as I wanted, or if I perceived it as "bad," my anger flared. And I stayed mad—not for a minute or an hour, but for as long as a day or a week, or maybe even for months or years. I allowed one negative situation to override all other aspects of my day, even the pleasurable, fun, and "good" events. I was unable to let go, forget, forgive, or move on. Unable to live "in the moment," my bad days outnumbered the good days. What types of things made me so mad, you ask?

- Dropping an object
- Getting stuck in traffic
- My husband's watching too much TV
- A client's cancelling a show
- The local radio station's changing the "time-saver traffic" report to "real-time" traffic
- Waiting in line at the grocery store
- Being put on hold on the telephone
- A store's discontinuing an item I frequently buy
- A rainstorm
- My husband's changing the radio channel when he drove my car and not changing it back after he arrived home

Do any of these things sound familiar to you? If you get mad over little things like those listed above, you are sweating the small stuff. After two years of therapy, listening to self-help CDs, and reinventing my thinking, along with the help of antidepressants, I've learned that everything in life is "small stuff." I no longer get angry or even become slightly irritated at any of the events listed above.

I live my life in a state of gratitude and know that the world and my day are not "all about me." In fact, it's not about me at all. Nor is it about you. We are all here on a journey, a mission; and everything that happens in my daily life is meant to happen, to teach me a lesson I need to learn in order to grow and become a better person. I am healthy and able-bodied; I have a warm bed to sleep in and a roof over my head, as well as good food in my refrigerator and pantry. I have all I need. (Material gains will never achieve happiness for anyone. A better car, more money, a better job, or being 20 pounds lighter will never buy a person's happiness.)

If you become irate or angered over small things, you may be suffering from a form of depression and often times may feel unhappy. If you do not realize you are unhappy, you could be suffering from a mood disorder.

Wonder how mad you are compared to others, or if you, too, might suffer from dysthymia? For a period of two weeks, write down everything that makes you mad every day. Also note how long you stayed mad and how mad you are on a scale of 1 to 10 (10 being totally and completely mad enough to act out in violence). After two weeks, look at your list. If your list consists of trivial, unimportant items that make no difference in your long-term happiness, or you stayed mad for a long time, it might be a good idea to seek counseling. I did ... and my quality of life improved tenfold.

Robyn Wheeler

Why Bad Things Happen to Good People

Like most people, you have probably asked yourself why bad things happen to good people. And you may never have gotten an answer you are satisfied with. But here's my theory:

The words *good* and *bad* are judgments—human judgments. For instance, I don't like being cold; therefore, in my opinion, snow is bad. But people who live back East and love to ski probably love snow and think it is great. Snow, in and of itself, is neither good nor bad; it just *is*. Human judgment is what deems something to be good or bad.

God doesn't judge. All people and things are considered equal. No one race, creed, or religion is good or bad, and no one person is good or bad or in between. God is neutral and all-forgiving. He created all of us with flaws and accepts those flaws. We humans are the ones who do not wish to accept our flaws or those of others.

So bad things don't happen to good people; rather, life happens to everyone. Bad things happen to good people and good things happen to bad people. In other words, everyone receives events and situations they perceive as bad or good, fair or unfair. Just because someone is a "good" person doesn't mean they escape this life without anything bad happening to them; just as "bad" people do not live their entire lives without anything good happening to them.

If you live every day, believing your life should be free from adversity, you are living with incorrect and unrealistic impressions of what life is all about. I used to be one such person; getting angry and saying, "It's not fair," when something I perceived as "bad" happened to me. The truth is, everyone has bad things happen to them. No one ever guaranteed us that good things would happen only to "good" people, and all the bad things in life would happen only to the "bad" people.

And besides, what criteria are used to define "good" or "bad" people? Are good people those who volunteer their time or money, give to others, always do what they are told, or have never been in trouble with the law? These things do not necessarily mean someone is "good." And what criteria are used to determine who is a bad person—jail, prison, homelessness, poverty, thieving, lying? These things don't necessarily label someone as "bad" either.

There is no such thing as a good or bad person. Again, this is an individual judgment based on your personal perception. All "bad" people have good qualities, and all "good" people have bad qualities. No one person is entirely good or entirely bad. We all have both good and bad traits.

God sees all of us equally. He doesn't love someone who has never committed a crime more than someone who is in prison for the rest of his or her life. He doesn't love nonsmokers more than smokers or rich people more than poor people. He loves everyone equally. No one is good or bad; we were all created equal, neutral, lacking judgment.

So next time you catch yourself saying something shouldn't have happened to someone because he or she is such a good person, stop yourself and remember: Life often deals us a bad hand; no one is exempt. We are not receiving a punishment for doing something wrong. We are just living life; a life with ups and downs, trials and tribulations, and happy and peaceful times as well. Our job is to take the hand of cards we are dealt and play the game as best we can with what we have. Good things happen to bad people and bad things happen to good people; that is just the way life goes here on earth. Peace and happiness come when we learn to accept the "bad" with the "good."

Robyn Wheeler

Pet Peeves

I don't have many pet peeves; at least I don't think I do. But here are some of them to start with:

1. Drivers who travel forward in the middle lane when they are trying to merge right. Not only is it illegal, it is just down right frustrating. Stop, people! You will eventually get to move right, but until the coast is clear, don't travel!

2. *Thru.* If you are writing something that is going to be read by another person(s) in a flier, brochure, book, etc., the correct way to write *through* is in fact, *t-h-r-o-u-g-h.* Not *thru!*

3. Animal owners who don't know how to care for their pet. Before you get a pet, whether it be a dog, cat, guinea pig, reptile, or bird, please research how to care for your pet. If you can't treat your pet like a member of the family, don't get one.

4. Smokers. Get with the times. Smoking is out; it is bad for your health and just a nasty habit. It's time to dump the cigarettes, including e-vapes.

5. Trophy hunters. We are losing our wildlife to the point of extinction, and still some ignorant folks wish to kill elephants, giraffes and others to hang their heads on a wall or make items out of it. Disgusting!

6. It irritates me to no end to be standing at the checkout counter at the grocery store, doing nothing, because I'm too far back to reach the only divider and the person in front of me is not considerate enough to pick it up and put it on after their own groceries. When I was a kid, my mom taught me to always put the plastic divider on the conveyor belt at the grocery store after the last

item was put on. That way, the person who comes behind you can start loading their groceries. It's just common courtesy, if you ask me.

7. The pinky finger that is always bent at the second knuckle even when it should be straight. Not the person's fault I realize, but it still creeps me out.

8. Those people who say, "Put Christ back in Christmas." If you are a Christian, then Christ never left your Christmas. If you are referring to those who are not Christian, it is none of your business and doesn't affect you at all if they don't celebrate Christmas. Only you can take Christ out of Christmas, and that is 100 percent your choice. Quit telling people to put Christ back in Christmas. What other people do is not your decision.

9. Feet. I hate feet. I hate looking at feet. Don't wear flip flops around me. I won't say anything to you if you do, but I will hate looking at your ugly feet. I've seen people with deformed toes, hammer toes, toes bending in different ways than they should. *Yuck.* I hate feet.

10. *Out of pocket* and *at the end of the day*. These phrases are being overused and drive me nuts. How can someone be out-of-pocket? What are you, a hamster?

11. Political jargon: rhetoric, narrative, nefarious, bad actor. What words did we use before we used "bad actor?" It seems a new slang or jargon crops up every week.

Okay, so I had more pet peeves than I thought. Do you have any of the same pet peeves I do? Maybe you have even better ones.

Choices

If you suffer from any form of depression, you have two choices. One, you can ask for help from a professional. Or two, you can live with depression hoping no one will notice and hoping it won't affect your life much.

The statistics are staggering. Over 40 percent of women do not seek help for depression, due to embarrassment. Over 50 percent of men with depression do not seek help due to fear of appearing weak. So, let's look a little deeper at the costs and benefits of the two options.

1. Even a mild depression can turn into a severe depression very quickly. Not only does depression hurt the person suffering from it, but their family and friends will be affected as well. Hoping that no one will notice is unrealistic. Someone is likely to suspect something. Depression is noticeable in many ways and on many occasions.

2. Depression is caused by a chemical imbalance in the brain. That is not your fault. It's not of your doing or of your choosing. You did not go to Walmart and buy a box of depression, take it home, and give it to yourself, like you would dye your hair or take a laxative. So why be embarrassed by something that is and was totally out of your control? As someone who spent over 40 years living with a mild depression, I am more embarrassed by those years than the years I've admitted to having dysthymia. Being diagnosed and getting treatment was the best thing to ever happen to me. It is not weakness to seek help when you need it—it is weakness *not* to seek help when you need it.

3. Everyday living with depression weakens you, your coping skills, and your ability to be a good parent,

spouse, or sibling. If you seek help and improve due to treatment, that's strength, not weakness. Seeking treatment for your illness will make you a role model, someone your family can look up to and turn to in tough times; someone whose actions they can follow. Not having enough respect for yourself and your family to seek help for an illness *is* weak and cowardly and arrogant.

4. A mental health assessment, prescriptions, and follow up visits can be expensive—but the emotional toll it will take on your everyday life if you don't take these steps will be immeasurable. The financial cost vs. the emotional improvement and stableness you will feel in your everyday life are incomparable. Before I was diagnosed, I would have given anything, whatever money it would cost, to find a cure. A cure would be priceless.

5. It's true that if you don't ask for help, you won't have to admit to your faults and your shortcomings. But "biting the bullet" and eventually "tucking your tail between your legs" and putting your ego aside might just be the best thing you ever do. It was for me. Admit your faults so you can learn and grow. Grow so you can be the person you were meant to be. Be the person you were meant to be because you are only here for a short while—make the most of it while you can.

Seeking help will do several things, among them:

- Improve your quality of life
- Prevent severe depression
- Improve relationships with everyone you know
- Allow you to feel real freedom

- Expand your horizons
- Help others

The list can go on and on. When you are happy, your perspective changes: you are emotionally stable, willing to try new things and meet new people, and you feel good about yourself and others.

You'll have to admit to your mistakes, misgivings and misperceptions. You'll probably feel terribly guilty at first, but those feelings will pass and you'll be able to move on to a better life, move on to a new and improved you.

So, which one do you prefer: A lifetime of denial and depression, feeling no joy and destroying relationships? Or would you rather set your ego aside, admit you need help, finding a treatment—the answers regarding what's been holding you back—and feeling better than you have ever felt in your life?

The choice is all up to you....

Just Call Me Firebucket

A Big Deal Out of Nothing?

Recently, one of my relatives told me that dysthymia is nothing more than a mild depression, that I should do my research and I was making a big deal out of nothing. Nothing? Depression is *nothing*?

Here's why I wrote *Born Mad* on this rarely talked-about disorder:

1. Mild depression can be just as detrimental and devastating to a person and their loved ones as a severe depression. At least 75 percent of people with dysthymia also suffer from another psychiatric disorder, such as anxiety disorder, OCD, drug addiction, or alcoholism. In and of itself, dysthymia can create havoc on a person's psyche and relationships, affecting everyone they know or encounter. But add to it one or two more untreated disorders—that's a recipe for disaster.

2. Individuals with dysthymia have a higher-than-average chance of developing major depression. This means, if you live with untreated dysthymia for any length of time, as I did, the chances are very good that you will one day sink to an all-time low, possibly even losing your will to live. What is so mild about that?

3. This mental disorder is genetic. If one member of your family is proven to have dysthymia, there is a strong possibility that others in your family are affected by it as well. Having one person in a family with dysthymia is bad enough, but having more than one or all members of a family with this disorder could spell disaster for the cohesion of the group.

4. Many men and women do not ask for help for depression, mild or severe. Yet 80 percent of all

people with any form of depression can be helped by medical treatment. That means, not only can a mild depression be devastating, but there is no reason for individuals to tolerate it as if it can't be helped. Seek help; find a treatment that works, and your life will turn around for the better. You will feel like a new person.

5. A major sign of dysthymic disorder is excess, chronic anger. Anger destroys. It destroys whatever and whoever comes along its path. Chronic anger and angry outbursts are never good. You will never make friends with anger— your own or anyone else's. Nothing more than mild depression, you may say? No such thing. Depression in any form is a mental illness and needs to be treated. You owe it to yourself, your family and friends, and everyone else you meet on a daily basis *not* to tolerate living with such a debilitating and life-long malady.

If you had diabetes, would you refuse to take your insulin? If you were diagnosed with cancer, would you refuse any and all treatments you might benefit from? If you had tuberculosis or Lyme disease or malaria, would you refuse treatment? I'm betting you most likely would do whatever possible to restore your health and well being. Mental disorders are no different. Please try anything and everything to help yourself and regain your sanity.

There is no such thing as "nothing but a mild depresssion." There is much more to dysthymia than a sad mood every now and then. Depression is depression. Please seek help so you won't have to live even one day of your life depressed.

Perception of the Mentally Ill

In 2011, I was diagnosed with a mental illness, a mild mood disorder called dysthymia. I wondered how people would see me, now I'd gone public with dysthymia? Would they think I was crazy? That I needed to be institutionalized? Or maybe that I was a criminal? None of the above was true, so how could it be that I had a mental disorder?

Read the following statements below and note how many you believe are true about mental disorders and the people who suffer from them:

1. People with mental disorders should be locked up in institutions.
2. Severe mental disorders are incurable.
3. People with mental illnesses are violent and dangerous.
4. With time, it will go away by itself.
5. Mental illness is a form of mental retardation.
6. Stress causes mental illness.
7. Mental illness is contagious.
8. "Poor parenting" causes mental illness.
9. Young people and children do not suffer from mental illnesses.
10. Mentally ill people can work low-level jobs but cannot handle really important or responsible positions.
11. People with mental illnesses are lazy and can get rid of it if they want to.
12. Only old people suffer from depression.
13. Only "weak" people suffer from mental illness.

14. Severe mental disorders are incurable.

15. A person with mental illness can never be normal.

All of the above statements are false. Surprised? If so, your perception of mental illness is outdated. According to the National Institute of Mental Health, more than 25 percent of the United States population suffers from a mental illness. Many receive treatment that makes them feel and act better than before. They could be your classmates, co-workers, neighbors, and even your relatives. That doesn't make them violent, crazy, or needing to be cared for in a facility. And it doesn't mean they cannot contribute to society, community affairs, education, or any other field. Even famous people suffer or have suffered from mental illness—people we admire, such as Carrie Fisher of *Star Wars*, comedian Howie Mandel, singer Michael Jackson, and economic and mathematical genius and Nobel Peace Prize winner John Nash.

All of the people mentioned above have or had a mental illness. And all of them have made tremendous contributions to their work, community, and friends and families. Even Mozart and Beethoven suffered from various types of mental disorders.

Society's perception, as a whole, of the mentally ill needs to change. Not all of us are locked up, confined to a bed or wheelchair or have drool running down our chin. (A small percentage of mentally ill *are* institutionalized, but most are not). Please treat anybody with a mental disorder with respect and admiration. Yes, *admiration*. For we are learning, growing, and trying to understand what makes us the way we are. Maybe one day, someone with a mental illness just might cure the very disorder they suffer from.

The Diagnosis

I wanted to die. I hated my life. I had a job I loved, a wonderful husband of thirteen years, and a beautiful house and loving family members. But all I could think about was crawling into a hole. My inner voices told me I was dumb, I couldn't do anything right, and I was worthless. How does someone get to be in their mid-40s and start thinking about committing suicide?

I went through two years of therapy with ups and downs and eventually called my therapist, begging for help. I cried and told her I would eat pot brownies, or undergo an exorcism or a lobotomy; anything, just to make the pain and misery go away. A week later, I was sitting in a psychiatrist's office hoping and praying the doctor would find something wrong with me that could be fixed or at least treated. After an hour of answering questions from "count down from 100 by sevens" and memorizing the words "rose, boat, house, tree" to whether I heard voices, and whether I thought someone was following me," help was on its way.

My husband was in the lobby, anxiously waiting to hear the news. I walked out and, as we approached the elevator, he asked me what the doctor said. "I have dysthymic disorder, and he gave me a prescription for Prozac," I replied. Neither one of us had never heard of dysthymic disorder. After I arrived home, I looked up dysthymic disorder on the internet to check out its symptoms and what kind of effects Prozac would have on me. I found out that dysthymic disorder is a chronic mild form of depression, now called *persistent depressive disorder*. Its symptoms include:

- Feelings of low self-worth, hopeless and emptiness
- Excess feelings of guilt
- Excess anger or angering easily
- Easily frustrated
- Inability to feel joy or excitement
- Overeating, or undereating
- Having thoughts of death or suicide
- Lack of problem-solving skills
- Insomnia or hypersomnia
- Poor concentration
- Social withdrawal
- Feelings of fatigue or low energy
- Chronic anxiety or worrying
- Moodiness

During my research, I found other facts about dysthymia including:

- Usually appears in childhood.
- Among those with dysthymia, 75 percent may have other disorders, including OCD, autism, Asperger's syndrome, etc.
- Dysthymia is genetic, and more women are affected by it than men.
- Dysthymia is often misdiagnosed as other forms of mental illness, including major depression and bipolar depression.
- Many doctors and psychologists have never heard of it and believe their patients are just complaining too much.

- Dysthymic disorder is a constant state of sadness. People who suffer from this condition have a low bar of happiness compared to others without the disease.

- Dysthymia sufferers are often seen as moody and are often overly critical, constantly complaining and incapable of having fun.

- Causes of dysthymia are complex and not completely understood. Some things that affect its onset include sleep abnormalities, hormones, neurotransmitters, upbringing, heredity, and stress.

- Among those with dysthymia, 80 percent can be helped by medication or other therapies.

As I looked at the list, it all made sense. It explains why I got kicked out of preschool for biting other children, why my job reviews said I was a hard worker but was moody and unapproachable. It explained why my boyfriends always dumped me and not the other way around, and why I got angry over little things and then stayed mad for a long time afterward. It also explained why, in 2005, I cried, screamed, and threw a temper tantrum because I had to have sinus and throat surgery. I panicked, acted like a child, and made everyone around me miserable.

After two weeks of taking Prozac, I felt better; and after three months, I felt like a different person. My perspective on just about everything changed. I was happier, hardly ever got mad, accepted God, and had better relationships with everyone I knew. My life became better. I had the same job, same husband, and the same house. All my circumstances were the same, except I took a pill every day. It amazed me how that one pill every day could change my life so drastically.

Since that day in October 2010 in the psychiatrist's office, I have written several books about dysthymic disorder, anger, and conquering depression, including *Born*

Mad, 104 Ways to Starve Your Anger and Feed Your Soul, and *The Dysthymia Diaries: True Stories of Living with Dysthymic Disorder and Finding Hope and Help.* I have spoken to small and large groups about what it is like to unknowingly live with mild depression and how it affected my life from childhood to the present time.

If dysthymia had been talked about when I was growing up, maybe I would have known sooner and gotten help sooner. I always thought I was normal; just like everybody else. When others told me I had a problem, I couldn't see it I blamed them and disregarded everything they said about me. It took thoughts of suicide for me to discover the truth.

Today, I believe the hell I went through before my diagnosis was one of the best things to ever happen to me. From all the pain, crying, depression, and unhappiness emerged a life I never imagined. My journey made me more compassionate and caring, less judgmental, and more tolerant of others. I have more patience, and now I laugh at things that, before 2010, would have ticked me off for days and weeks.

I found the real "me"—the "me" that was hiding beneath the depression, beneath the anger and low self-esteem. I thought I was being weak and fragile, but my husband saw courage and determination. My struggles and lowest point in life made me the person I am today. It gave me strength to fight another day and make my future as happy as it can be.

Dysthymia is not curable. I've had it all my life and will continue to have it. It is caused by an imbalance of serotonin in the brain and other chemicals that regulate mood, control of anger, and happiness.

Although dysthymia is not curable, it is treatable with the help of medication, self-help techniques, affirmations, and learning new ways of coping with stress and improving on problem-solving skills. The biggest influence on my health today, other than medication, is listening to and reading the work of Dr. Wayne Dyer, a prominent psychologist and spiritual guru. His tapes and books taught me how to change my attitude, ditch my neurotic behavior, and learn to live in the moment.

Most women are stronger than they know or give themselves credit for. We often say "I can't get through this," or "This will destroy me." The fact is, many women get through some horrible, unspeakable trials. Louise Hay was abused as a young child in unspeakable ways. Today, she is the owner of Hay House, one of the largest self-help, inspirational, and transformation publishing and radio companies. She survived, wrote dozens of books, and spoke of her childhood in order to help others. And you can too.

I believe our trials and tribulations make us stronger. I believe we are given these challenges to make us better people, to allow us to grow emotionally, spiritually, and mentally, and to help others who may be going through similar circumstances. The pain clarifies our thoughts and strengthens our will and constitution. Without pain, growth would come to a screeching halt. The trick, for all of us, is to figure out why these things happen as we are going through them, what we need to learn from them, and how we can use what we have learned.

Remember, the reason for your pain will appear. Maybe not at that moment, maybe not even a month after, but it will appear. Try to tell yourself that your circumstances are temporary, there is a better way to live and you have the strength to get past it, move on, forgive, and live the life you were meant to live.

Don't be afraid to remember where you came from and all the hard times you went through. Remembering where you came from will increase your gratitude for what you have today.

I see and know many people who make "a mountain out of a molehill," criticize others for something they can't possibly know anything about, and degrade others around them. I used to do all of those things too. But having sunk to my lowest point brought new feelings, attitudes, perspectives, and compassion. I no longer care whether the draperies in my house match the carpet, or what my neighbor does with his or her life. I no longer believe I need a bunch of material things or have to have a lot of money. I appreciate the small things and all the nice things others do for me. I forgive everyone, including myself, and I try to see others' point of view.

Along the way, I hope I can help others with what I have learned and overcome; to help others gracefully deal with the bad times as well as the good. Perhaps you have heard the saying, "Be kind to others, always, even if you don't like them, for everyone you meet is fighting a harder battle."

You are not alone. Others have been through and survived the challenges you face. It is never too late to ask for help. Asking for help takes courage, and many of us dislike asking others for help. Sometimes it just takes one person to open their heart and door to another human being, to make a difference in the world. Making a difference in the world comes about, one person at a time. Never lose hope. Fight for the person inside you, and fight for your freedom. You are worth it.

Just Call Me Firebucket

Syndromes You Didn't Know Existed

Being a curious person and growing up in Southern California, I have only been out of the country once, in 1994 to Costa Rica and England. So I am often curious as to other cultures, customs, and beliefs in other countries or areas of the world. While I was reading the *Diagnostic and Statistical Manual of Mental Disorders, Fourth Edition*, or DSM-IV-TR (I'm not crazy, just fascinated by unusual disorders), I ran across a glossary of culture-bound syndromes. I thought I would share some of them with you because maybe I'm not the only one who never knew they even existed.

- **Ghost sickness** is often associated with witchcraft and is a preoccupation with death and the deceased and is commonly observed in many American Indian tribes. Various symptoms can be attributed to ghost sickness, including bad dreams, weakness, feelings of danger, loss of appetite, fainting, dizziness, hallucinations, confusion, and sense of suffocation.

- **Hwa-byung** or **wool-hwa-byung** is a Korean folk syndrome that means "anger syndrome" and is attributed to the suppression of anger.

- **Koro** is a Malaysian term that refers to an episode of sudden and intense anxiety in which the penis will recede into the body and then cause death.

- **Amok** is a dissociative episode characterized by a period of brooding followed by an outburst of violent, aggressive, and homicidal behavior directed at people and objects. This behavior pattern is found only in males residing in Malaysia, Polynesia, Philippines, Papua New Guinea, Puerto Rico, and among the Navajo.

- **Pibloktoq** is an abrupt dissociative episode accompanied by extreme excitement of up to 30 minutes' duration and frequently followed by convulsive seizures and coma lasting up to 12 hours. During the attack, the individual may tear off clothing, break furniture, shout obscenities, eat feces, flee from protective shelters, and perform other irrational or dangerous acts. Pibloktoq is found primarily in the arctic and subarctic Eskimo communities. (Maybe it's the subzero temperatures that make them crazy—I know it would me!)

- **Susto** is a folk illness among some Latinos in the United States, Mexico, Central America, and South America. It refers to an illness attributed to a frightening event that causes the soul to leave the body and results in unhappiness and sickness.

- **Taijin kyofusho** is a distinctive phobia in Japan that refers to an individual's intense fear that his or her body, its parts or functions, are displeasing, embarrassing, or offensive to other people in appearance, odor, facial expressions, or movements.

- **Zar** is a general term applied in Ethiopia, Somalia, Egypt, Sudan, Iran, and other North African and Middle Eastern societies that refers to the experience of spirits' possessing an individual. Persons possessed by a spirit may experience shouting, laughing, hitting their head against a wall, singing, weeping, apathy, and withdrawal.

- **Spell** is a trance state in which individuals "communicate" with deceased relatives or with spirits and is associated with periods of personality changes. Spells are not considered to be medical in nature but may be misconstrued as psychotic episodes in clinical settings. Seen mostly among

African Americans and European Americans from the southern United States.

- **Brain fag** is a condition seen in West African high school or university students in response to the challenges of schooling. Symptoms include difficulties in concentration, remembering, and thinking; also head and neck pain, pressure or tightness, blurring of vision, and/or heat or burning. Students often state their brains are "fatigued."

Robyn Wheeler

Santa Kills Six

My Christmas was sad but good. I had a nice warm meal, spent time with my family and friends, and received several gifts. It was sad, without my grandmother. She had been my last living grandparent and died one month after her 100th birthday in June 2011. This was my first Christmas without a woman who has been in my life for more than forty years; but even so, I will always remember it as a good Christmas.

But December 25, 2011, will always be remembered by another family in Texas—not because it was good, but because it was horrific and unexpected and just shouldn't have happened to any family any day of the year, much less on a cherished holiday. Early Christmas morning, a man in Grapevine, Texas, dressed in a Santa Claus suit, shot and killed six of his relatives and himself. Family members were opening presents when this "Santa" decided, for reasons known only to him, killed four women and two men in their home. And now the only thing anyone can do is pray for the victims and their families and for an end to this kind of tragedy.

Will humans ever find a solution to murder and suicide? As someone who has had some family members succeed with their suicide wishes and others attempt but, thankfully, not succeed, I believe we all need to band together to end depression once and for all. If you know someone who you suspect is depressed, please offer your help. Be willing to do whatever is in your power to help them help themselves. Support in the form of a shoulder to cry on and an ear to listen to may be all they need to realize the truth.

Depression hurts everyone, no matter what form, mild or severe. Some medication works, some doesn't, and some wears off in a short time. The same is true for non-pharmaceutical approaches. Don't get mad at the person.

For if they have gotten to the point of murder or suicide, they are not thinking clearly, nor do they have the emotional strength to get through it by themselves. And they do, most likely, believe they are all alone and that no one understands. Have compassion, sympathy, and understanding. Forgive the ones who committed the heinous, unthinkable act, and love them for who they are or were. They are or were, after all, someone's child, father, mother, sibling, or other loved one, and they were loved by others.

We all have tough times, emotional setbacks, and hurdles to face. Remember the worst time in your life and understand that a person who is willing to commit murder or suicide is much worse off than you can probably understand. Send love, peace, and forgiveness to all, every day. My loved one was not here for Christmas, and many other families are suffering a similar loss.

At present, all we can do is try to help those still here on earth and continue to find ways to fight anger and depression. If you or anyone you know is contemplating murder or suicide or both, please call 9-1-1, the depression hotline at (630) 482-9696, or the suicide hotline at (800) 784-2433. Do it for all of those who lost loved ones throughout the years. Blessing and peace on earth to all.

Robyn Wheeler

The Ohio Man
February 2012

As a 15-year veteran wildlife animal keeper and educator, and as someone who has in the past contemplated suicide, I have two very different points of view regarding Terry Thompson, the Ohio man who freed more than 56 wild animals and then shot himself.

First, let's start with the release and killing of the animals. As an avid animal lover, I deplore the fact that these priceless and possibly sick or injured animals were released.

Many people who do not want their pets or exotic animals make the mistake of releasing them back into the wild, believing the animals will be better off in their natural habitat, that they will fend for themselves and will be just fine. The flaw with that thinking is the most animals raised in captivity do not know any other way of life. When released, these animals don't know how to either hunt or escape from predators, and they do not know what a gun, rifle, or car looks like. Many possibilities can become a reality, and most of them do not have a happy ending. These newly released animals that have lived in captivity for most or all of their lives eventually starve to death, fall prey to a predator within a short amount of time, or trust humans, which they wouldn't normally do, which leads to being hunted, shot, or hit by a car.

Anyone in the wildlife industry should know better, especially someone caring for potentially dangerous and aggressive animals such as monkeys, lions, tigers and/or bears. Also, here in the United States, we do not have native habitats for such animals as kept by Thompson, so these animals face even greater odds of death, not to mention the loss of 18 endangered species. That is a price we all will pay for generations to come. If these animals were unwanted or no longer needed, they could have been given to rescue groups, zoos, or animal rehabilitators. They did not have to die.

Now, let's to go the side of a person who is depressed, who is not thinking clearly or logically, and who has had notable emotional issues in the past. As someone who has considered suicide, I can speak only for myself. When I was depressed and lost interest in living, I was not concerned about others—animal or human. I was concerned only about myself and could not get past pitying myself and my situation. I didn't care what my family or friends would go through if I killed myself. I was unable to think or empathize with how my actions might affect others.

If, Terry Thompson had any kind of mental illness that carries with it any form of depression, anxiety, anger, frustration, or, worse yet, hallucinations or hearing voices, he was not in a position to be rational, logical, or reasonable. He thought only of himself and could have even been completely convinced, himself, that freeing these animals was the right thing to do.

It's unlikely Thompson thought of the consequences—someone's getting hurt or contracting Herpes (a disease transmitted by animals to humans or the reverse), the animals' being shot or killed, and the environmental impact of releasing endangered animals that cannot be kept as a pet by most humans. If Thompson was emotionally or mentally unstable at the time, his greatest concern was taking his own life.

And if someone contemplates taking their own life, why would anyone expect that same person to be concerned about animals—any kind of animals? Maybe he truly believed that since he was living in hell and wanted out, life for the animals had to be hell as well. As a wildlife educator, many parents called me asking if I had a monkey or alligator or lion, because their small child was just fascinated with them and wanted one at his/her birthday party. I explained that I never carry those types of animals because most are not suited for "show and tell," much less being poked and pulled on by toddlers.

These animals are dangerous even for the best and most highly skilled and educated wildlife experts. Even Siegfried and Roy were victims of finding out what strength tigers are capable of. Currently, I do not know of any law making it illegal for someone with a mental disorder or past conviction history to own wildlife, unless they may have previously been convicted of animal abuse/neglect. Nor is there an "adoption" process for owning such animals. People who own zoos, wildlife, or exotic pets don't have to pass a mental assessment before ownership is approved. And many exotic animals, like lions and tigers and bears, are sold and purchased on the black market.

Yes, a permit is required, but some folks won't pay the money and keep the animal illegally until they get caught, which could be days, weeks, months, or even years. The message our society should take away from this tragedy is also twofold. One, we need better and more affordable mental health care in America so even those in the lower income bracket can afford counseling, psychiatry, and prescription renewal. And two, the acts of one or two individuals should not result in a law that punishes the masses.

If the actions of Terry Thompson results in a ban on exotic animal ownership, shouldn't there have been a ban on guns after Columbine or Virginia Tech? From what I've seen and heard in the media in the past decades, it seems that those with mental disorders can also own rifles and shotguns.

Stories

Robyn Wheeler

Just Call Me Firebucket!

When I was about three years old, my godparents nicknamed me "Firebucket." Just by the sound of it, you know this can't be good, right? Well, it wasn't.

As a young child, my family frequently went to my godparents' house for dinner or the holidays. My godparents had four kids, all about the same age as my sister and I, and we liked to play together while the grownups chatted about the latest events and details of their lives.

One day, my sister and godsiblings ran out the front door to go to a neighbor's house. Of course, as is true of all small children at that age, I wanted to do everything the older kids did. But they considered me a nuisance, a tag-along little kid, so they sped out the front door so fast that it slammed closed in my face as they giggled and ran off.

My godparents lived in a large, two-story, five-bedroom home with extremely heavy double front doors. My parents said that I had, in the past, opened the doors by myself. This time I stood there screaming. My face turned red. I yelled at my folks, who were busy chatting. They could see me at the front door with my tiny fists tightly clenched, yelling at the top of my lungs.

I remember thinking I couldn't open the door, and I was upset that everyone had left without me. Being excluded and left behind was no fun. As a three-year-old, I didn't know what to do other than cry. My parents and my godparents continued with their conversation, taking a brief timeout to tell me to open the door and go outside.

After about five minutes of screaming, yelling, making fists, and stomping my feet on the ground until I was red-faced, my tantrum became entertaining for the grown-ups. My godfather said to my folks, "Wow, you got your hands full with this one!" Everyone laughed and joked that my face was bright red and thought if I could have blown fire from my mouth or nostrils, I would.

Just Call Me Firebucket

Again, my godfather piped up, saying, "She's just a small bucket of fire, isn't she?" And there it was, my nickname: *Firebucket.*

Robyn Wheeler

That Little Girl with the Snake

One of my favorite memories involves startling a hospital orderly when I was four years old. I had been hospitalized for a few days to undergo tests for severe stomach pains. One time, my parents showed up for their daily visit with a plastic snake that, when held by its tail, would sway back and forth like a real one. I enjoyed playing with the snake and couldn't put it down.

My prankster father had a plan and instructed me to stand up against the wall just inside my room and wait for his cue. When he gave me the cue, I was to hold the snake outside the doorjamb just long enough for someone to believe it was a real snake. So when Dad gave the cue, I held the snake by its tail and stuck the snake out the door into the hallway and then I heard it: a loud shriek and fast footsteps. As peered out the doorway. I saw only a large cluster of towels piled on the floor.

My family was laughing hysterically, and I had no idea why. It turned out my father had waited until a female orderly with a fresh load of clean towels came down the hallway on her way to the linen closet. When she was just a few feet from the door, my father gave me the cue to put the snake in the hallway. The orderly, who turned out to be deathly afraid of snakes, screamed, threw her hands up in the air, and ran the other way. She then told the nurses and doctors that a wild dangerous snake was loose on the hospital floor.

Eventually, the hospital employees got wind of what really happened and, for the next three days, the hallway was empty. In fact, the crew flipped a coin to see who had the task of bringing the food tray to "the little red-headed girl's room."

Just Call Me Firebucket

The *Los Angeles Times*

Yep, that's me. On the Front Page, above the fold in the Jun 22, 1992 Orange County issue of the Los Angeles Times. I was volunteering at Friends of the Sea Lion Marine Mammal Center at the time, and we got a call of this poor pup out on the rocks. So I drove out to Laguna Beach with a few other volunteers. We got out our nets and put on our slickers, and I walked out into the waves with my net. I thought the pup would go back into the ocean before I could snag him, but he stayed right there and was easy to capture. I don't remember what we named him, nor if he was ever returned to sea once he was back on his feet—well, flippers—again. But that was the only time I made the front page of a paper. They must have had a slow news day, or the photo was too good not to publish.

The article that accompanied the photo said:

> Two volunteers last Monday afternoon struggled to rescue a sickly sea lion that clung to a jagged rock at Crystal Cove State Beach. They sloshed through the surf, wrestled their slippery catch into a net and dragged it onto shore.
>
> Despite the animal's writhing, which twisted the net into a snarl, the workers got the 45-poound pup into a cage and hoisted it onto a pickup truck for a trip to the center.
>
> "Believe me, I am tired and soaked up to here," Robyn Battershill, one of the volunteers, said before climbing into the truck bed next to the sand-caked sea lion. "It's real difficult to get them off a rock like that. A lot of times we lose them and they go back to the ocean."

Just Call Me Firebucket

Oh, Skunk!

I worked as an animal control officer in Orange County, California, for two years, from 1994 to 1996. One day, while on shift, I got a call about a skunk in a lady's back yard that had a Yoplait yogurt cup stuck on its head. I responded, and the woman took me into her back yard to find, sure enough, a skunk walking around in circles with a Yoplait yogurt cup stuck on its head. Now saying it was a Yoplait yogurt cup is important here because these cups are narrow at the top and wide at the bottom. It seems this poor skunk was rooting through the trash and got his head inside the yogurt cup; but then when he tried to pull his head out, the cup narrowed and the poor thing couldn't get free. I don't know how long he was stuck inside the cup. If only cell phones had been available back then to film it; I would have liked to submit my footage to *America's Funniest Home Videos* but I don't believe AFV was on the air at that time either.

So, I got my catch-all (the long pole with the wire hoop on the end) and put it over his head. He was easy to catch as he couldn't see me coming! This happened in San Juan Capistrano, and the lady lived at the base of a mountain. So I used the pole to walk the skunk across the street to the base of the mountain. Then I tugged on the yogurt cup until it came off and quickly released the skunk from the catch-all. I thought he might try to spray, so I backed up quickly. However, the skunk just took a look around and then sauntered off up the mountain. He didn't try to spray or be aggressive, he just walked away. Lucky me.

The view of that poor skunk is the funniest thing I saw during my two years as an animal control officer, and I will probably remember it for as long as I live.

Robyn Wheeler

Grilled Children

So, working at a newspaper is always interesting, especially when terrible errors are made. We had one reporter, who, on the top of the front page, wrote "Spiffy Headline Goes Here." Well, it passed the proofreading phase and went directly to press. The next morning, the front page read "Spiffy Headline Goes Here."
But that's not the funniest. Let me explain.

It was August 4, 2013, and I was told to go to a new Mexican restaurant in the area and do a write up. I went to the restaurant, took photos of the owners, got a take-out menu so I could write about some of their plates when I got back to the office, and took a photo of a plate of food—a taco plate or something. I wrote my article and turned it in, but my editor didn't like it. And instead of having me rewrite it or make improvements based on her suggestions, she wrote the article instead. She went to the restaurant, took photos of about five different dishes, and went back to the office to write a lengthy article about the food they served.

She went on to explain several of their dishes in depth, including the Grilled Chicken Salad.

She wrote, "Sweet Salad offers grilled children over crisp Romaine lettuce, strawberries, blackberries, diced apples, dried cranberries almonds and walnuts dressed in Raspberry vinaigrette." Did you catch it? "Grilled children"? Yep, it too, passed the proofreading stage and was sent to press saying "grilled children."

The funny part was we made the *David Letterman Show*. He has a segment called "Small Town News." And yep, about a week after the paper came out, David Letterman read the goof-up on his show. I don't know who turned it in to the *David Letterman Show*, but you have to admit "grilled children" is a hell of a mistake!

Just Call Me Firebucket

Joe Smith

Who is Joe Smith? Joe Smith (name has been changed) is a man who lives at Cedar Creek Lake and called the newspaper to speak to a reporter. That reporter just happened to be me. He wanted to vent and complain about a few city officials he spoke to who did not give him what he wanted. So I talked to him for what I thought was more than enough time, listening to him as he told his story. He repeated himself more than two or three times, and after about 15 minutes I thanked him for the information and told him I had to go. He ignored me and continued to ramble on about his problem. Again, I stated I was busy and had to get back to work. He hung up on me. I have published a letter he wrote to *The Monitor*. The questions I had for him were more than just a punctuation mark; and, yes, his fourth-grade level of spelling needed clarification on many levels. Here is what he wrote:

> *Commentary dated October 3rd, 2014:*
> It was earlier this week I submitted to the Monitor newspaper out of Athens, Texas, a "Letter to the Editor" for possible publication in the forthcoming Sunday paper. It was headed "What is a Registered Voter in Gun Barrel City?" The submitted letter was followed up by a correction e-mail to one punctuation error in the prior Letter submitted, which was followed up by a phone call to me by a volunteer/employee who claimed to be a Reporter of the Monitor who did not understand my fourth-grade reading level letter.
>
> The woman who claimed to be reviewing my letter was looking for a reason, I believe to reject the letter. She was one of those over educated idiots from the liberal establishment who had no concept of what a true reporter is all about. What makes it worse the woman actually has a business in the area attempting

to teach others proper communication when it comes to anger issues. I hung up on her.

Earlier this week the mid-week Monitor paper related the resignation of the EDC Board President, Linda Rankin and Councilman, Curtis Webster. Both of these resignations indicate the failure of both the City Council in general and the city manager of GBC to play a true leadership role in the development of GBC. As to the Council itself, its greatest self-server Marty Gross needs to be removed from the council.

Any individual who is a realtor or developer should never qualify to be on any city council, in any city in Texas. The same applies to being on appraisal boards for counties in Texas. As to our City Manager, eight years is long enough to hold that position for any city manager. Of course, I guess if he stays on, we can rename Gun Barrel City, "Boren Country."

The forthcoming GBC elections in November 2014 is an attempt to insure that bringing city taxes to GBC will insure the $140,000 year salary, plus vehicle, plus expenses, plus a fat retirement for GBC city manager, Gerry Boren and maintaining the private rest room in his individual office at GBC city hall. Following is the copy for submitted letter that was to be printed, but more than likely will not be printed:

Subject: Letter to the Editor of the Monitor paper of Athens, Texas

Title: What is a Registered Voter in GBC?

Dear Editor,

As eight-year lake front owners and permanent residents of Gun Barrel City, we have observed purposeful misdirection of what constitutes a registered voter in Gun Barrel City by the city administration. When we contacted the city of GB via their Facebook website, their response was follows when we inquired as what the definition of a qualified voter was in GBC, their response was, "A Resident is as defined as a fixed place of habitation."

Some of the misstatements in the past rendered to me by GBC city officials was that one must be a homeowner with a "Homestead Exception" filed on their home. I was told the same when I was entertaining volunteering for the Economic Development Board. This is an untruth, a "Homestead Exception" is not required to vote in GBC elections.

A renter qualifies to be a registered voter in GBC. Another misstatement was that your driver's license must reflect your GBC address. Requesting a "Resident Statement" at the location you are voting at, takes care of this problem. The residency requirement is a simple six months. One can obtain a voter registration card showing their GBC address by simply calling the Voter Registration Registrar in Athens, Texas at 903-675-6160. As to our positions on the upcoming city tax elections in November, we are voting "No" to new city taxes.

First, the *Monitor* is based in Mabank, not Athens. Second, I was not looking to reject the letter, I would never do that. But I couldn't publish the letter the way it was written. **And third, he hung up on me, so maybe he needed to take one of my anger management courses.**

Here are the emails he wrote to my boss:

Oct. 1, 2014

Dear Sir/Madam,

I have just hung up from a telephone call from your reporter Robin Wheeler, you reporter with the Monitor, regarding my recent submittal and correctional email for "Letters to the Editor Page" this coming Sunday. From my fifty years experience in sales, sales marketing and being the owner of several successful businesses, I found Ms. Wheeler both rude and without any real understanding of what a true news reporter is all about.

You can do yourself and big favor and avoiding the negative impression Ms. Wheeler gives other in her communications with others regarding the Monitor paper, by calling her in to your office today and terminating her. Again, from my experience a complaint such as mine indicates the "tip of the iceberg" when it comes to reporting a poor employee/volunteer?

Sincerely Yours,

Joe Smith

Oct. 4, 2014

Cancel my prior letter submittal of a letter to the editor. I wish to remove any possibility of the letter being published at a later date in your paper. The reason for the request are many but mainly because of lack of professionalism of your Ms. Wheeler who would not make a pimple as a reporter on the ass of an ant. I thought the letter was going to the publisher of the paper and not the jack leg reporter who called me earlier this week regarding my letter.

Joe Smith

And no, I didn't get fired. It seems many others at the paper had had negative experiences with this man, so most of us just laughed and brushed him off.

Just Call Me Firebucket

Happy Easter! Happy Easter! Happy Easter!

In August 2005, my allergist informed me I needed to undergo a procedure to clean out my clogged sinus cavities, remove a large wart on my uvula (the small piece of flesh hanging in the back of the throat), and remove my tonsils. Terrified at the idea of being put under anesthesia, I fell apart. After four years of allergy shots, numerous bouts of tonsillitis, and a wart that started out as the size of a pea when I was thirteen but had grown to the size of a grape, making swallowing difficult, my health would not improve without surgery.

My husband's birthday was the day before my surgery. I sulked all day, talked to my sister and my mother, and felt like I was saying goodbye to everyone. I cried most of the day, and it was the first year that we didn't celebrate my husband's birthday. We stayed home all day while I cried and threatened to back out of having surgery.

I was convinced something bad would happen during my surgery and I would be scarred or even die, but my husband tried to calm me down and talk some sense into me. But inside, I was angry and depressed and felt like my life was being turned upside down. I became immobilized with fear. Today, I look back on this and wish my family had realized how neurotic I was and insisted I see a therapist. But no one thought I had a problem with neurosis, fear, or anger.

Early the next morning, my husband drove my mother and me to the outpatient center located about an hour away from my home. While sitting in the waiting room at 6 a.m., I cried until I couldn't cry anymore, begging my husband not to make me have surgery. I screamed, fought, and argued, pleading with anyone who would listen to take me home. At one point, my husband actually did offer to take me home.

But I knew surgery was my only hope. For years, my sinuses had been clogged with old, hardened mucus, and it was becoming impossible for me to clear my passageways when I had an allergy attack. Stuffed up all night and all day, forced to breathe through my mouth, I had numerous coughing attacks due to a dry throat, and no medication on the shelves seemed to alleviate the problem.

So, I hesitantly stayed, following the nurse down the short hallway to the dressing room, where she instructed me to take off my clothes and jewelry, put on the gown, and wait for her to take me to a bed. Once in the bed, my mother and my husband were allowed to keep me company, and I was crankier than ever before.

A small child, most likely an infant or a toddler, kept crying on the other side of the curtain. She was obviously scared, too, and needed comfort from her parents. She had some kind of toy to help keep her calm, which kept repeating "Happy Easter! Happy Easter! Happy Easter!" After about five minutes of listening to this child cry and yell, I bitterly remarked, "Just one more happy customer, huh?" And I don't believe you really want to know what I threatened to do with the toy!

Eventually, the anesthesiologist came in and spoke to me, and I responded in a bitter and mean tone. I told him to make sure they removed my uvula and not the female body part that's spelled similarly. He injected me with some cocktail and in about a minute, I was feeling good, laughing and joking. When the stretcher pulled away, taking me down the hallway to the surgery room, I commented about needing an "E ticket" to get on the ride. (This was a Disney reference from when individual tickets were distributed for particular rides instead of one all-day pass good for all attractions.)

The surgery took more than an hour, but it seemed like a minute to me. I woke up with cotton stuck up both nostrils and a nurse forcing crushed ice down my throat. I remember constantly pushing her hand away because, when I closed my mouth to swallow the ice, I couldn't breathe. I kept refusing the ice, and she kept insisting I swallow it.

My mother helped the nurse put me back into my street clothes, and I was wheeled out to the car. I could hear my husband and my mother conversing, and I wanted to talk but couldn't get any words out. They laughed on the drive home about my being so quiet and subdued. Those were the first moments of peace either one of them had enjoyed in several days. To this day, they both claim they will never forget that ride home and the "Happy Easter!" toy.

Robyn Wheeler

Pot Brownies

If you read *Born Mad*, you know that I told my counselor I was ready to try pot brownies if it would make me feel better. I did eventually try pot brownies, but not for depression.

I have never tried any drugs, not even cigarettes. But in my late 40s I gave pot brownies a try. I was having terrible back pain for days, actually weeks. Nothing I took was touching my pain. I took hydrocodone, iced my back, and took Advil and Tylenol. I was still writhing in pain. I could not sleep, just tossed and turned. I thought my pains were from arthritis.

One day I was talking to a neighbor who said she buys pot in Dallas and makes brownies and I should try one. So I said, "Why not?"

She gave me four brownies and told me, "Take one, and if it doesn't work in about an hour, take another one." I took a brownie one day I was home and didn't have to go anywhere because I had no idea how I would react to it. I felt nothing. About a week later, I thought this time I would eat two. I ate one, nothing happened. I forgot about the suggested one-hour time lapse in between and ate another one about 10 minutes later. Boy, did I regret that decision.

I was afflicted by every side effect known to man. I was paranoid and had hallucinations. I was telling my husband that I had done permanent brain damage to my brain and I would never be normal again. I was shaking, and my husband told me to lie down. I fell asleep for minutes at a time; and every time I woke and went back to sleep, I was having the same dream, and each was shorter and quicker than the previous one. My heart was pounding; I felt like I was going to throw up and fell into and out of consciousness. My throat and neck, as well as the left side of body and face, were numb. I thought I'd had had a stroke. My husband called the neighbor and she came over, but there was nothing she could do except apologize. I don't remember how long this lasted; probably a few hours. After the pot wore off, I was back to normal. All I wanted was pain relief, not to get high.

The next day, I gave her back the pot brownies and took to the internet to see if I could find any information on reactions to pot brownies. Boy, did I. I found several people who wrote about their bad pot experience. I also found out if you've never tried pot before you should smoke it, not eat it. Edibles take longer to kick in, but they also last longer. Also, pot is made from weeds (hence the name) so if you are allergic to weeds, the kind in your yards that have pollen and wreak havoc on your sinuses a few times of year, don't do weed! I am allergic to pollens. Just about every weed out there makes my sinuses run like crazy. So, if you are allergic to ragweed, chickweed and other weeds, stay away from "weed."

My first time doing drugs will be my last time. As far as legalizing pot, I've known a lot of people who are in favor of it and say it cures their headaches, seizures, and other disorders. I don't know if I'm for legalizing it, but right now Colorado and California have already done so. Thank God I don't have permanent brain damage from the experience.

Robyn Wheeler

You're on the Air

After *Born Mad* was published, I was a guest on quite a few radio and television stations. Some were fun, some weren't, and some were strange. Here's one of the strange ones.

I got an email from a man who wanted me to be a guest on his radio show. It was a short letter, and it struck me as odd because he signed off with just his name and no station identification. But I wrote back I would be a guest, and we arranged for a date and time. So I called in and he answered, still not giving the station identification. Then he put me on hold. This is fairly common, but I must have been on hold for at least five minutes and the music that was playing was heavy metal, to say the least—lots of screaming, yelling and loud guitar.

When he came back on the phone, he asked me if the Boston Marathon bombings made me mad. (The bombings had happened earlier that day.) I said, "No, it was sad, but if I get mad it won't do anyone any good so there is no point in being mad." He pressed the issue a few more times, stating they were based right about where the bombings took place. I still maintained that, no, I was not angry; I would let the authorities handle it. Then he proceeded to tell me they worked in a small room with no air conditioner and they were hot. So, I gave them some suggestions, like getting a fan, buying an air conditioner, and speaking with their landlord about the situation, and they balked at all my suggestions.

Then they put me on hold again. When they came back, they said they had someone who wanted to speak with me and when the man spoke, he had a lisp and kept calling me "Wobyn." Now, the man's voice, to me, sounded exactly like the host, only with a lisp. So he kept calling me Wobyn, and by this time the red flag in my head was raised. So, I decided to turn the tables and ask some questions of them. I asked how many listeners they had, if they put listeners on the air to ask questions, and how long the show had been on the air. I think I made them nervous; and by the time I got done asking questions, they hung up on me.

Now, my red flag was telling me these guys were trying to make me mad. Kind of a weird goal, but between the loud music, the Boston Marathon questions, the rejection of all my ideas about their room, and the man with the lisp, I pretty much thought this was a gag. I even asked them if this was a gag. They hung up soon after.

I'd never encountered another interview like that before, nor did I ever find this interview published anywhere on the internet. Again, they hung up on me, so maybe they, too, could use a little anger management.

Robyn Wheeler

Comedy Speech

I give a lot of speeches about my disorder, and the mood in the room can get a little "depressed" by talking about depression. So, in an attempt to lighten the mood, I wrote a comedy speech where I make fun of myself. This is my speech.

* * * * *

Thank you for allowing me to speak today. Many of you have heard me speak before, so I thought I would share a few things about me you may not know.

Firebucket

I was born in California with bright red hair sticking straight up on my head and a really bad temper. By the time I was two, I was known as Firebucket. My family was visiting my godparents' house and I was playing with my sister and god sister when they ran outside. I was too slow, and the door slammed closed in my face. I stood at the door screaming and crying, my hair was sticking up on end, my face was beet red, and my fists were clinched. I stomped my feet on the ground. If I had had smoke billowing from my ears, I would have looked like Yosemite Sam after failing to catch that pesky rabbit. My godfather took one look at me and said, "Well, isn't she a big bucket of fire?" And there t was. My nickname for at least the next ten years. Firebucket was my name, tantrums were my game!

Biting

When I was four, I was expelled from preschool. Whenever I got frustrated or cranky, I would grab hold of a classmate's arm and sink my teeth in as hard as I could. I'm not sure how many victims I had altogether, but I found this poster in the post office:

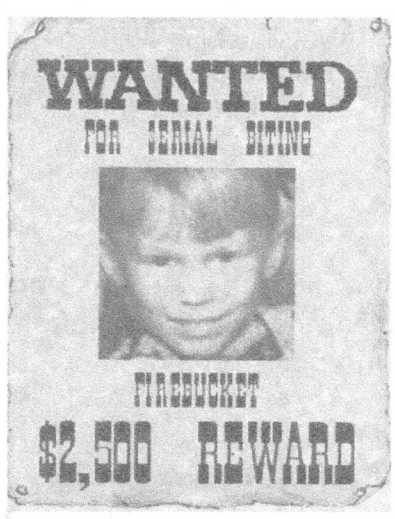

Photo used in my comedy speech.

When I die, my headstone will probably say "Youngest Juvenile Delinquent Ever."

Most spiritual leaders say successful people look at a situation with a positive attitude. It's not what happens to a person, it's what a person thinks (positively) about the event. So here is a list of positive things about my being a biter:

- Ten years later I had to get braces, and the dentist said, "I need you to sink your teeth into this gooey, bitter tasting goop." Hey, no problem—I've been doing that since preschool!

- My parents saved a bunch of money because they didn't have to get a guard dog. They just posted a "Caution, Biting Child" sign on the fence, and everyone stayed away.

- The kids in preschool will never forget me because I made a lasting impression on them.
- If I ever need another job, I have quite the résumé: I could try out for the lead in a vampire movie; I could always be Sergeant McGruff, the "Take a Bite Out of Crime" dog.

You're probably wondering if I grew out of it. Yes, shortly after that I lost my taste for meat. When I used to go to Catholic Church with my husband, at the end of every service, before communion, the priest would say everyone should drink Christ's blood and eat his flesh (wine and bread). No way, not me. I can't see how Christ's flesh tastes any better than the 4-year-olds at the Scarred for Life Preschool in California.

Hospital

When I was five, I was hospitalized for a mystery stomach pain. The next day in the hospital my parents brought me a toy snake. I loved animals even then, so to me this was the funniest thing ever. My father, being a practical joker, told me to stand up against the wall by the door jamb and, when he gave me the say-so, to stick the snake out the door, not revealing myself. So, he gave me the signal, I held the snake by its tail, making it wiggle back and forth, and then I heard screaming and footsteps running down the hall. My father was cracking up, and I looked around the door jamb to see a pile of towels scattered all over the floor and no one to be seen. It turned out my father waited until he found a woman from housekeeping walking down the hall with an armload of clean, freshly folded towels.

From then on, the nurses, housekeeping, and food staff avoided the fourth floor. I think they must have drawn straws, thrown dice, or flipped a coin to see who had to go to the little red-headed girl's room. My parents should have purchased the floor and put a statue of me out front, calling it the Serpentine Wing, "Beware of Snake Ghosts of Past." I think my parents had to take me home a few days later for fear I was going to starve to death in the hospital. Maybe if they had told the doctors I was a biter, my mystery stomach pain wouldn't have been such a mystery. But the doctors never asked if I was a relative of Hannibal Lecter.

Today

Today, I am a newspaper reporter, an anger management coach, and the author of several books about overcoming chronic anger. People often ask me, "Why should I take anger management classes from you when you have anger issues?" I reply, "I don't have anger issues—I don't, I don't, I don't!" Anger management is actually very simple. It all boils down to changing your attitude. Many folks who take my classes are unable to see another person's perspective. They need to understand others do things differently than they do.

    I will use myself as an example. I grew up in Southern California and was in the snow only about three times growing up. I was miserable each time and still to this day have no idea why anyone enjoys being in the snow. Do you know some people actually pack a bag and board a plane to take a vacation on the top of a mountain? Then, these same people pay money to be carried up a slope, so they can slide down at top speed, all in an attempt to avoid large stationary trees? If they don't crash, they do it again!

    My definition of hell is not standing by a nice warm fire. My definition of hell is sitting on a bucket in an ice shanty in Minnesota waiting for my next meal to decide it doesn't want to live anymore. And don't tell me God created the Emperor Penguin either. Only the devil would make a large flightless bird slide on its stomach buck naked on layers of frozen tundra to lay one egg and battle blistering blizzards for months on end, only to trample the poor little chick and then call it nature.

Mental Illness

In all seriousness, I do want to discuss the state of how the mentally ill are treated in this country. In December 2012, the nation mourned for 20 children and six teachers who were shot to death in Newtown, Connecticut, by a 20-year-old with Asperger's syndrome and autism who shot himself in the head. And rightly so, to mourn for the dead, as this was a terrible tragedy.

But I've heard no one express grief over Adam Lanza, who was also a victim. He was a victim of a mental illness which he did not ask for or want. He didn't go to Walmart, purchase a box of autism and take it home and administer it to himself like person would a hair dye. The day of the Newtown shooting, I heard an internationally known psychiatrist on her national radio show say that people like Adam Lanza "shoot others for fun and entertainment. They do things like that because they like to, they get a rush from it." I disagree wholeheartedly with that statement. I believe they get to that point because they are miserable. They feel unheard, unseen, unloved, and forgotten. They fall into the cracks, they receive little or no attention for their mental differences, and no one makes the time to find out what is bothering them. Adam Lanza didn't wake up one morning and decide to kill people. He most likely had been depressed, angry, and empty for some time.

Gun control is not the issue we should be discussing. We should be discussing making psychiatry free of charge and putting psychiatrists in every school in the U.S. When I wrote *Born Mad*, I wrote about wanting to start a charity to help others pay for prescription medications. Since I began speaking about mental illness in 2011, I've met several people who said they were forced to go off their meds because they couldn't afford them. We should not be afraid of those who are taking their medication; we should be afraid of those who aren't.

Adam Lanza was also a victim of poor mental health care in this country. Psychiatry is extremely expensive, and many rural areas do not have qualified mental health practitioners, leaving some folks to drive for at least an hour to find a psychiatrist. Prescription medications are expensive. I pay almost $200 a month for my medication which is equal to two weeks' pay for me. I'm fortunate because I have a husband who finds ways to "skimp" on other things rather than on my medication.

Mental illness is not 100 percent of who someone is. It is only a part of who we are. Underneath the illness, beneath the symptoms of bipolar, depression, and schizophrenia, is a loving, smart person filled with potential. Before you use words like *crazy*, *looney*, *bonkers*, and *psycho*, please remember that a person with feelings, desires, and emotions is inside. The more people use these terms, the fewer people will seek help for fear of being ridiculed or trashed by their family and friends. It is estimated that 24 percent of Americans have a mental illness. However, the National Association of Mental Illness feels a more accurate number is probably around 44 percent. So, what accounts for the other 20 percent? The stigma surrounding mental illness that scares others from seeking help.

Conclusion

Those of us with mental illness cope the best we can. We don't get angry or walk the streets naked talking to an invisible person about government conspiracy theories because we can't think of anything else we'd rather be doing.

To end on another humorous note, I have thought of positive sides to having a mental illness:

- I'm too busy dealing with my own problems to worry about yours.
- I have an excuse for doing and saying off-the-wall things.
- I don't have to ask myself if I've "lost it."
- I get to take happy pills.
- I don't need you to laugh at me—I can do that myself.
- My husband can say, "If you think I'm crazy, you should meet my wife!"

About the Author

An avid animal lover since childhood, Robyn Wheeler created a wildlife education company in 1996 called The Creature Teacher, LLC. Based in Northeast Texas, Robyn traveled throughout the state, presenting various animal-related shows to children and adults of all ages at local schools, libraries, and birthday parties. She graduated from California State Polytechnic University, Pomona, in 1988, worked at Disneyland as an animal caretaker for eleven years, and was an Orange County Animal Control Officer for two years. Before starting her own business, she taught an animal-care class to high school students for the Regional Occupational Center of Garden Grove. Robyn now lives on nine acres with her husband, Ron, and calico cat, Zoey.

2019

Robyn sold The Creature Teacher in 2011 and moved to Gun Barrel City on a half acre of land. Robyn has written two more books: *104 Ways to Starve Your Anger and Feed*

Your Soul and *The Dysthymia Diaries: True Stories of Living with Dysthymia and Finding Help and Hope.*

Robyn continues to be a radio and television guest and gives presentations in and around Northeast Texas.

Born Mad is receiving 5-star ratings on Amazon and has received several local awards.

Robyn has also published *The Creature Teacher Frog-tastic Funbook* series for children.

Robyn is also a Certified Anger and Stress Management Facilitator and a Certified Equine Sports Massage Therapist.

www.ingramcontent.com/pod-product-compliance
Lightning Source LLC
Chambersburg PA
CBHW071407080526
44587CB00017B/3205